MICROSOFT

WORD

2024

THE MOST UPDATED AND COMPLETE GUIDE FROM
BEGINNER TO ADVANCED USERS

CHARLES SHERER

TABLE OF CONTENTS

INTRODUCTION   6

CHAPTER ONE   7

QUICKNESS METHODS FOR USING WORD   7

PRESENTING THE WORD SCREEN   7
BUILDING A NEW DOCUMENT   8
OBTAINING A BETTER LOOK AT YOUR DOCUMENTS   10
CHOOSING TEXT IN SPEEDY WAYS   13
NAVIGATING AROUND QUICKLY IN DOCUMENTS   14
PUTTING A WHOLE FILE INTO A DOCUMENT   18
OBTAINING WORD TO READ IT   18
DOCUMENTING INFORMATION FASTER IN A COMPUTERIZED FORM   19

CHAPTER TWO   21

SPREADING OUT TEXT AND PAGES   21

PARAGRAPHS AND FORMATTING   21
PUTTING IN A SECTION BREAK FOR FORMATTING GOALS   21
BREAKING A LINE   23
BEGINNING A NEW PAGE   23
SETTING UP AND CHANGING THE MARGINS   23
INDENTING PARAGRAPHS AND FIRST LINES   24
NUMBERING THE PAGES   27
PLACING HEADERS AND FOOTERS ON PAGES   30
MODIFYING THE SPACE BETWEEN LINES   33
MODIFYING THE SPACE BETWEEN PARAGRAPHS   35
CONSTRUCTING NUMBERED AND BULLETED LISTS   37

CHAPTER THREE   42

WORD STYLES   42

USING STYLES TO TEXT AND PARAGRAPHS   43
CREATING A NEW STYLE   47
MODIFYING A STYLE   48
BUILDING AND MANAGING TEMPLATES   49
MODIFYING, DELETING, AND RENAMING STYLES IN TEMPLATES   52

CHAPTER FOUR   54

CREATING THE EXCELLENT TABLE   54

CREATING A TABLE   54
ENTERING THE TEXT AND NUMBERS   57
CHOOSING DIFFERENT PARTS OF A TABLE   58
LAYING OUT YOUR TABLE   58
ALIGNING TEXT IN COLUMNS AND ROWS   62
MERGING AND SPLITTING CELLS   63
FORMATTING YOUR TABLE   64

CHAPTER FIVE   70

TAKING BENEFIT OF THE PROOFING TOOLS AND INDEXING A DOCUMENT   70

CORRECTING YOUR SPELLING ERRORS   70
CORRECTING GRAMMATICAL ERRORS   73
FINDING AND REPLACING TEXT   73
CONDUCTING A FIND-AND-REPLACE OPERATION   75
FINDING THE RIGHT WORD WITH THE THESAURUS   76
PROOFING TEXT WRITTEN IN A FOREIGN LANGUAGE   78
TRANSLATING FOREIGN LANGUAGE TEXT   79

CHAPTER SIX   80

DESKTOP PUBLISHING WITH WORD   80

INVESTIGATING WITH THEMES   80
NEATENING UP YOUR PAGES   81
MAKING USE OF PHOTOS, SHAPES, DIAGRAMS, AND CHARTS   85
WORKING WITH THE DRAWING CANVAS   85
WRAPPING TEXT AROUND AN OBJECT   87
WORKING WITH TEXT BOXES   89
DROPPING IN A DROP CAP   91
WATERMARKING FOR THE ELEGANT EFFECT   92
LANDSCAPE DOCUMENTS   94
PRINTING ON DIFFERENT SIZE PAPER   95
DISPLAYING ONLINE VIDEO IN A DOCUMENT   95

CONCLUSION   97

INDEX   98

INTRODUCTION

Welcome to Microsoft Word 2024, an efficient tutorial that imparts you everything you need to know about Microsoft Word to remain current, creative, and self-assured. This mini-book will teach you how to use MS Word's most helpful and amazing features in a stress-free. You will learn how to insert and format shapes, photos, tables, and charts, you will also discover how to create, edit, and format a document from the ground up like a professional. Microsoft Word, popularly called **MS Word,** or **Word**, is a word-processing application established by Microsoft Corporation. The majority of important Microsoft Word features have been around for a long time and the basics remain constant over all editions. Continue reading if you have an older version of Word, Word 2021, or Word 2019; this mini-book will be very useful to you. MS Word permits you to create, edit, format, save, and print business documents, including books, bills, reports, graphics, email, notes, certificates, and more. It features a simple user interface and it is very stress-free to use. If you want to start using Microsoft Word, you must have it installed on your computer or use it online.

CHAPTER ONE

Quickness methods for Using Word

This chapter describes shortcuts and commands that can assist you in becoming a swift user of word 365. In this chapter, you will learn how to construct and modify your view of documents. You will discover how to choose the text and move from place to place, you also examine how to insert one document into another.

Presenting the Word Screen

Viewing the word screen for the very first time may be something confusing and intimidating. But when you begin to use Word, you speedily learn what everything is. To assist you, the image below displays the diverse aspects of the screen.

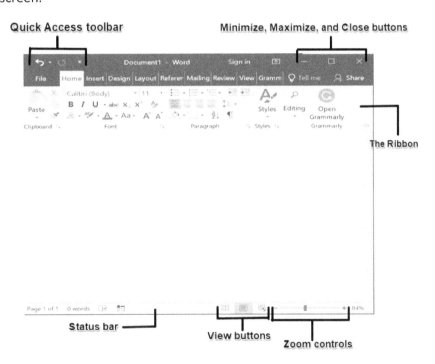

Here are shorthand explanations of those screen aspects:

> ➤ **Quick Access toolbar:** The toolbar provides the AutoSave and Save button.

- ➤ **The Ribbon:** Choose a tab on the Ribbon to launch a new job. Tab names-file, Home, insert, and a lot more- are found along the top of the Ribbon.
- ➤ **Minimize, Restore, Close buttons:** These buttons make it very comfortable to expand, compress, and close the window you are working in.
- ➤ **Status bar:** The status bar provides you with fundamental knowledge about where you are and what you are doing in a document. It gives you information on the page what section you are in, and the total number of pages and words in your document.
- ➤ **Zoom controls:** Use these controls to zoom in and out on your work.
- ➤ **View buttons:** To modify your view of a document, click one of these buttons- Read mode, Focus Mode, Web Layout, or Print Layout.

Building a New Document

Document is another word for letter, report, proclamation, or announcement, that you construct with Word. All documents are built using a unique kind of file named a template. The template supplies the formats-the fonts, styles, layouts, and so on, that provide a document its formation.

Follow these steps to build a document:

1. **On the File tab, select New.** The New window appears.

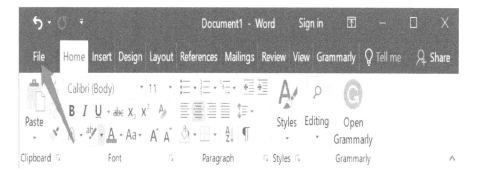

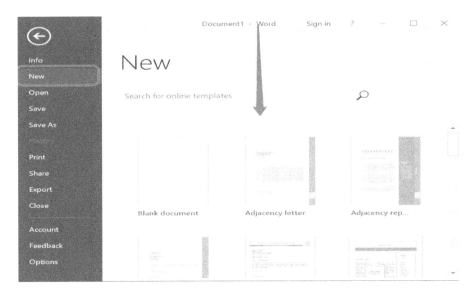

2. **Click to choose a template.** A preview window displays with an explanation of the template you selected.
3. **Click the Create button.** Your new Word document unlocks.

Apply these methods in the New Window to select a template and create a document:

> ➤ **Select the Blank Document template:** Select Blank Document to create a naked document with a handful of styles. (press Ctrl+N, to create a new document without unlocking the New window.)

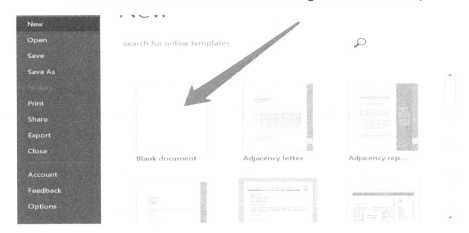

➢ **Search online for a template:** Input a search term in the Search box and click the Start Searching button.

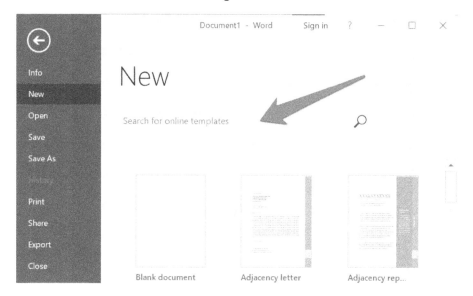

➢ **Select a template:** Choose a template to explore it in a Preview window. Then click the create button in the preview window to build a document from the template.

➢ **Select a personal template:** On the personal tab, click to choose a template and build a document. A personal template is one you built or copied to your computer or network. If you have one it will display.

Obtaining a Better Look at Your Documents

A computer screen can be kind of Restricting. Glancing at a damnable thing for a long time. Do you desire the view to be satisfactory? You can explore documents in diverse ways and work in two places at a time in the same document. Just continue reading.

Viewing documents in diverse ways

To assist you staying in focus, word provides diverse ways of viewing a document which are:

- Read Mode

- Print Layout
- Web Layout
- Outline
- Draft
- Focus Mode

Changing views

Apply these methods to change views:

- ➤ Click one of the four buttons on the right-hand side of the status bar.
- ➤ Select the View tab, and click one of the five buttons in the Views group or the Focus button in the immersive group.

Read mode

Change to Read mode to concentrate on the text itself and proofread your documents. You cannot input or edit text in Read mode. Everything is deprived away- the scroll bars, status bar, ribbon, and all. All you can view are the text and artwork in your documents. Read mode is created for reading documents on tablet computers. To exit Read mode, click View on the menu bar at the top of the screen and select Edit Document on the drop-down menu.

Web Layout view

Change to Web Layout view to notice what your document would look like as a web page. Background colors display (if you select a theme or background color for your document). Text is enveloped to the window rather than around the artwork in the document.

Print Layout view

Change to Print Layout view to view the big image. In this view, you can view what your document will look like when you print it, you can click the one Page, Multiple Pages, or Page Width button on the View tab to show more or fewer pages on your screen. You can see clearly where page breaks occur and you can also view graphics, footers, headers, and page borders in Print Layout view.

Outline view

Change to Outline view to notice how work is organized. In this view, you can notice only the headings in a document. you can also discover how your document unfolds and easily shift sections of text backward and forward in a document.

Draft view

Change to Draft view when you are writing a document and you want to concentrate on the words. Shapes, pictures, and other distractions don't show in this view, nor do page breaks.

Focus Mode view

Change to Focus Mode view to make reading a document comfortable. This view is created to prevent eyestrain. You can input text in Focus Mode view, all editing commands text are deprived from the screen. Press the Esc key to exit the Focus Mode view.

Splitting the screen

You can be in two places at a time in a Word document by splitting the screen, besides opening a second window on a document. follow these steps to split the screen:

1. **Click the Split button on the View tab.** A gray line displays onscreen.
2. **Drag the gray line till the gray line is where you wish the split to be.** You obtain two screens split down the middle. Another way to split the screen is by pressing Ctrl+Alt+S.

Choosing Text in Speedy Ways

After you input text, you unavoidably have to copy, move, or delete it, but you can't carry out those jobs until you select it first. Table 1-1 explains shortcuts for choosing text.

Table 1-1   Shortcuts for Choosing Text

To choose this	Do this
A line	Click in the left margin next to the line.
Some lines	Drag the mouse pointer across the lines or drag it down the left margin.
A word	Double-click the word.
A sentence	Ctrl+click the sentence
A paragraph	Double-click in the left margin next to the paragraph.
A mess of text	Click at the beginning of the text, hold down the Shift key, and click at the end of the text.
A gob of text	Place the cursor where you wish to start choosing, press F8, and press an arrow key, drag the mouse, or click at the end of the selection.
Text with the same formats	On the Home tab, click the Select button and pick Select Text with Similar Formatting but you may have to click the Editing button first.
A document	Hold down the Ctrl key and click in the left margin; triple-click in the left margin; press Ctrl+A; or move to click the Select button, and pick Select All, but you may have to click the Editing button first.

Viewing the hidden format symbols

Sometimes it is good to view the hidden format symbols when you are laying out a document and editing it. The symbols display line breaks, paragraph breaks, tab spaces, and the spaces between words. To view the hidden format symbols, visit the Home tab and click the Show/Hide ¶ button, click the button again to hide the symbols.

Here is what the hidden symbols look like onscreen.

Symbol	How to Enter
Tab (→)	Press Tab key
Space (.)	Press the spacebar
Optional hyphen -(-)	Press Ctrl+hyphen
Paragraph (¶)	Press Enter

Navigating Around Quickly in Documents

Beyond sliding the scroll bar, Word provides a handful of very speedy methods for navigating around documents. Continue reading to know how to get there faster.

Keys for moving around quickly

One of the quick ways to move from place to place is to press the keys and the key combinations listed in the table below.

Key to press	Where it takes you
PgUp	Up the length of one screen
PgDn	Down the length of one screen
Ctrl+PgUp	To the previous page in the document
Ctrl+PgDn	To the next page in the document
Home	At the start of the line
End	At the end of the line
Ctrl+Home	To the top of the document
Ctrl+End	To the bottom of the document

Moving from heading to heading or page to page

The best way to move from place to place is to make do with the Navigation pane. You just need to click a page or a heading in the Navigation pane, and Word will land you there immediately. To show the Navigation pane, visit the View tab and click the Navigation Pane check box (you may need to click the Show button first). Then choose a tab in the Navigation pane and move to it:

> **Moving from heading to heading:** Choose the Headings Tab. Headings in your documents display. You can use the Navigation pane like a table of contents and select the headings to move from place to place.

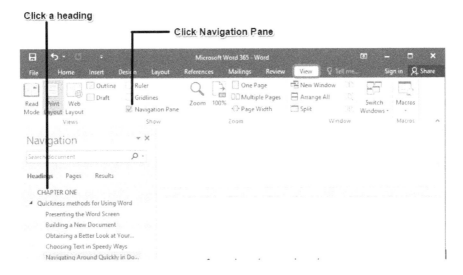

> **Moving from page to page:** Choose the Pages tab. A thumbnail picture of each page in the document is displayed. To move quickly from page to page, make use of the scroll bar in the Navigation pane or click a page thumbnail.

Click a page thumbnail

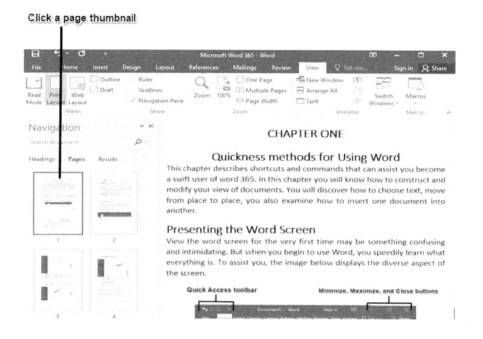

Moving there fast with the Go To command

Another way of moving from place to place in a document is to make use of the Go To command. On the Home tab, unlock the drop-down list on the Find button and select Go To (you may need to click the Editing button first). You notice the Go To tab of the Find and Replace dialog box, displayed in the image below, you can also unlock this dialog box by pressing Ctrl+G or F5.

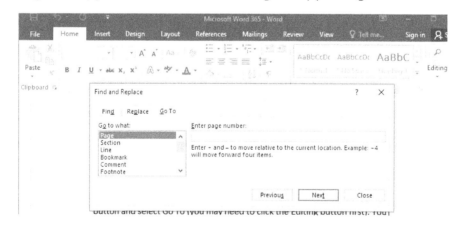

The Go-To What menu in this dialog box outlines all that can be numbered in a Word document, and other things, too. Click a menu item, input a number, select an item from the drop-down menu, or click the Next, previous, or Go To buttons to move to some other place.

Bookmarks for moving around

Another quick way of navigating around in a document is using bookmarks, all you need to do is to put the bookmark in an essential place in your document that you will get back to many times. See the bookmark dialog box below:

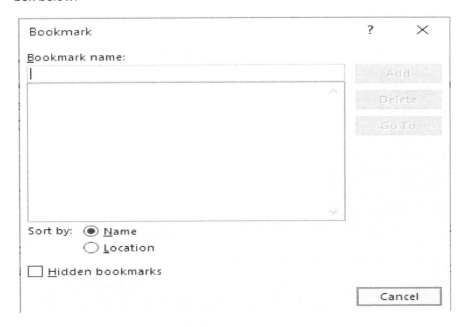

Follow these steps to deal with bookmarks:

> **Inserting a bookmark:** Select where you want the bookmark to go, click the insert tab, then select the bookmark button (you may need to click the Links button first, depending on your screen size). So, in the bookmark dialog box, type a descriptive name in the Bookmark Name box, and click the Add button. Bookmarks cannot begin with numbers or include blank spaces.

- ➤ **Going to a bookmark:** On the Insert tab, click the Bookmark button, double-click the bookmark in the Bookmark dialog box, then click the Close button.
- ➤ **Deleting a bookmark:** Choose the bookmark in the Bookmark dialog box and click the Delete button.

Putting a Whole File into a document

One of the amazing things about word processing is being able to reclaim documents. Follow the steps below to put in or insert a whole file into a document

1. **Position the cursor where you want to insert the document.**
2. **Click the insert tab, unlock the drop-down menu on the Object button, and select Text from File.** You notice the Insert File dialog box. (The Object button can be found on the right side of the Ribbon in the Text group).
3. **Find and choose the file you want to insert.**
4. **Click the Insert button.**

You can insert more than one file with the Text from File command. Choose more than one file in the Insert File dialog box then click the Insert button. Files drop in the document in the order in which they show in the Insert File dialog box.

Obtaining Word to Read It

You can make Word to read it aloud, without you reading it yourself. Follow these instructions to hear Word read part or all of a document:

1. **Unlock the document that needs to be read.**
2. **Change to Print Layout view or Web Layout view, if essential.**
3. **Click the Read Aloud button on the Review tab.**
4. **Click the stop button on the toolbar or the Read Aloud button a second time to make Word stop reading.**

Documenting Information faster in a Computerized Form

A form is a way of recording and pleading for information. These pages describe how to create a form and use it to record information. The first step in creating a data-entry form is to build a template for holding the form. The next thing to do after that is to design the form itself by labeling the data fields and constructing the data-entry controls. Keep on reading.

Creating a template to hold the form

Follow the instructions to create a new template:

1. **Press Ctrl+N to create a new template.**
2. **On the File tab, select Save As.**
   You notice the Save As window.
3. **Click the Browse button.**
   The Save As dialog box unlocks.
4. **Unlock the Save As Type menu and select Word Template.**
5. **Enter a descriptive name for your template and click the Save button.**

Building the form and data-entry controls

Your next job is to construct the form and data-entry controls for your template. Input labels on the form where you will impute information. After you input the labels, follow these instructions to construct the data-entry controls:

1. **Show the Developer tab, if essential.**
   In case the tab is not showing, visit the File tab, select Options, and on the customize Ribbon category of the Word Options dialog box, search for the Developer check box on the right-hand side of the screen, choose this check box, and click OK.
2. **Select where you wish to place a control, and then create the control by clicking a Controls button followed by the Properties button on the Developer tab.**

See the instructions for creating three types of controls below:

- **Combo box:** As with a drop-down menu, a combo box "drops" to display choices. Click the Combo Box Content Control button, then the Properties button. In the Content Control Properties dialog box, impute the option names.
- **Drop-down list:** A drop-down list is a menu that drops when you unlock it to display diverse option choices. Click the Drop-Down List Content Control button and then the Properties button. You notice the Content Control Properties dialog box. For every option you want on the drop-down list, click the Add button, and in the Add Choice dialog box, input the option's name in the Display Name text box and click OK.
- **Date picker:** A date picker is a mini-calendar from which data-entry writers can input a date. Click the Date Picker Content Control button and then the Properties button. In the Content Control Properties dialog box, select a display format for dates and click OK.

3. **Click the Save button to save your template.**

Entering data in the form

Since you now have the template, you can impute data cleanly in easy-to-read forms by following these instructions:

- ➤ **On the File tab, select New.**
- ➤ **Click the Personal tab.**
  This tab displays templates stored on your computer.
- ➤ **Double-click the name of the template you created for entering data in your form.**
  The form displays.
- ➤ **Impute information in the input fields.**
  Press Tab and Shift+Tab or the up or down arrow to navigate from field to field. You can also select an input field to move the cursor there.

20

Chapter Two

Spreading Out Text and Pages

This chapter describes how to format text and pages. It also presents tricks, tips, and methods for making pages look just right. You will learn in this chapter what section breaks are and why they are so essential to formatting, you will know how to inaugurate the size of margins, number pages, indent text, determine how much space shows between lines of text, text, handle text, construct headers and footers.

Paragraphs and formatting

Talking about a paragraph in word processing is simply what you put on the screen before you press the Enter key. For example, a heading is a paragraph. If you press Enter on a blank line to move to the next line, the blank line is assumed a paragraph. If you type **Dear Janet** at the top of a letter and press Enter, "Dear Janet" is a paragraph. The paragraph is very important in word processing because paragraphs have a lot to do with formatting. If you click the Paragraph group button on the Home tab and navigate around with the paragraph formatting in the Paragraph dialog box, your changes affect everything in the paragraph where your cursor is placed.

Putting in a section break for formatting goals

If you want to modify headers and footers, page-numbering schemes, margin sizes, and page orientations in a document, you need to construct a *section break* to begin a new section. Word constructs a new section for you when you construct newspaper-style columns or modify the size of margins.

Follow these steps to construct a new section:

1. **Select where you what to insert a section break.**
2. **On the Layout tab, click the breaks button.**
   You unlock a drop-down list.
3. **Beneath Section Breaks on the drop-down list, choose a section break.**

The image below displays what the diverse Section breaks look like. All four section break options construct a new section, but in a diverse manner:

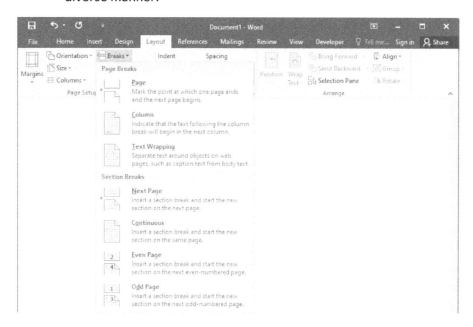

➢ **Next page:** Insert a page break and a section break so that the new section can commence at the top of a new page (the next one). Choose this option to begin a new chapter, for instance.

➢ **Continuous:** Inserts a section break in the middle of a page. Choose this option if, for instance, you want to introduce newspaper-style columns in the middle of a page.

➢ **Even Page:** Commences the new section on the next even page. This option is good for two-sided documents in which the headers on the left-side and right-side pages are different.

➢ **Odd Page:** commences the new section on the next odd page. You might select this option if you have a book in which chapters begin on odd pages.

To delete a section break, be certain that you are in Draft view so that you can view section breaks, click the dotted line, then press the Delete key.

Breaking a line

Press Shift+Enter to break a line of text before it gets to the right margin without starting a new paragraph.

Beginning a New Page

When you fill-up one page, Word provides you another page so that you can keep going. but if you are impatient and want to begin a new page instantly, you don't have to keep pressing the Enter key. Instead, just create a hard page break by applying one of the following on the insert tab:

- ➢ Click the Blank Page button. Word enters two hard page breaks to create an empty, blank page at the cursor position.
- ➢ Click the Page Break button. Word begins a new page at the cursor position. You can also visit the Layout tab, click the breaks button, and select Page on the drop-down menu.

Setting Up and Changing the Margins

Margins are the blank spaces along the right, left, top, and bottom of a page, you can put text boxes, graphics, and page numbers in the margins. Margin framed the text and made it comfortable to read. See the image below.

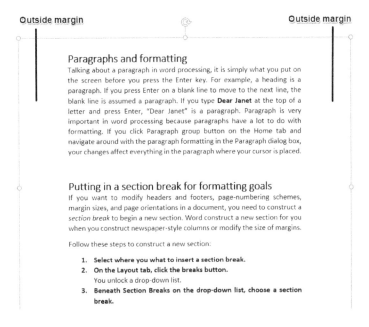

To set up or modify a margin, visit the Layout tab and click the Margins button. The drop-down list with margin settings appears. you have the choice to select a setting on the drop-down list or choose Custom margins to unlock the Margins tab of the Page setup dialog box and select among these commands below for handling margins:

➢ **Making room for the gutter:** The gutter is the aspect of the paper that the binding eats into when you bind a document. Input a measurement in the Gutter box to increase the left or inside margin and make room for the binding.

➢ **Changing the size of the margins:** Enter measurements in the Left, Right, Top, and bottom boxes to inform Word how much space to put along the sides of the page.

➢ **Applying margin changes:** On the Apply To drop-down list, select Whole Document to apply your margin settings to the full document; select This Section to apply them to a section; or select This Point Forward to modify margins in the rest of a document. When you choose This Point Forward, Word creates a new section.

➢ **Using mirror margins (inside and outside margins) in the two-sided document:** Select Mirror Margins on the Multiple Pages drop-down menu and modify the margins consequently if you plan to print on both sides of the paper.

If you are impatient to change margins, you can modify them on the ruler. Show the ruler by selecting the Ruler check box on the View tab. Then drag the Left Margin, Right Margin, or Top Margin marker. You can locate these makers by shifting the pointer onto a ruler and searching for the two-headed arrow near a margin boundary. It displays, along with a pop-out label when the pointer is across a margin marker.

Indenting Paragraphs and First Lines

The distance between a margin and the text is known as an indent. Word provides a handful of ways to modify the indentation of paragraphs. You can modify the indentation of the first lines and also the entire paragraphs. To begin, choose all or aspects of the paragraphs you desire to re-indent. Then click an indent button, wiggle with the indentation marks on the ruler, or move to the Paragraph dialog box. All the three methods are explained here:

Clicking an indent button (for left-indents)

Click the decrease Indent or Increase Indent button on the Home tab, or press Ctrl+M to shift a paragraph a half-inch farther away from or nearer to the left margin. If you built tab stops, text is indented to the next or prior tab stop and also to the next or prior half-inch. This is the quickest way to indent text, but you cannot indent first lines or indent from the right margin this way.

"Eyeballing" it with the ruler

You can also modify indentation by applying the ruler to "eyeball" it. To do this, visit the View tab to show the ruler and click the ruler check box.

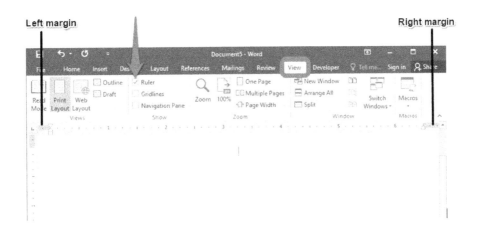

Then click in or choose the paragraph(s) that require indenting and apply these methods to re-indent them:

> **Indenting the whole paragraph from the left margin:** Drag the left-indent marker on the ruler to the right. Dragging the left-indent marker shifts the first-line indent marker as well.
> **Indenting the first line of a paragraph:** Drag the first-line indent marker to the right. This marker decides how far the first line of the paragraph is indented.

➢ **Indenting the whole paragraph from the right margin:** Drag the right-indent marker to the left.

➢ **Making a hanging indent:** Drag the hanging indent marker to the right of the first-line indent marker.

Indenting in the Paragraph dialog box

An alternative way to indent a paragraph or first line is to visit the Paragraph dialog box, as displayed below:

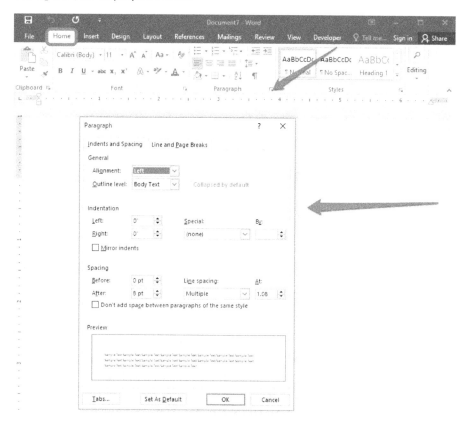

Choose the paragraph or paragraphs in question, move to the Layout or Home tab, and click the Paragraph group button. You notice the indents and spacing tab of the Paragraph dialog box. Modify the indentation settings. For example, if you want to create a hanging indent or indent the first line, select First Line or Hanging on the Special drop-down list and input a measurement in the By box.

Numbering the Pages

Your document can be numbered in sequence beginning with the number 1, start numbering pages with a number apart from 1, use Roman numerals or other number formats, and incorporate chapter numbers in page numbers, when it comes to numbering pages, you can move in two ways:

 ➢ Include the page numbers in the header or footer.
 ➢ Put a page number by itself on the pages of your document

After you have input a page number, you can format it in diverse ways in the Page Number Format dialog box, and Headers & Footer Tools Design tab.

Including a page number in a header or footer

To insert the page number part in a header or footer, double-click in the header or footer where you wish the page number to display. Then follow these instructions to insert the page number:

1. **On the Header & Footer tab, pick the Page Number Button.**

2. **Select Current Position.**
   You notice a submenu with page number options.
3. **Scroll through the submenu and select a page number format.**

Numbering with only page numbers

Follow these instructions to insert a page number by itself in the header, footer, or margin of the pages:

1. **Visit the insert tab, then click the Page Number button.**

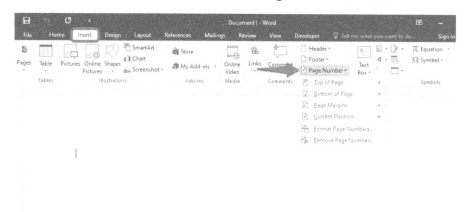

2. **From the drop-down list that appears, select where on the page you want to put the page number either the Top of the page, the bottom of the page, page margins, or Current Position.**
3. **On the submenu that comes into sight, select a page number option.**

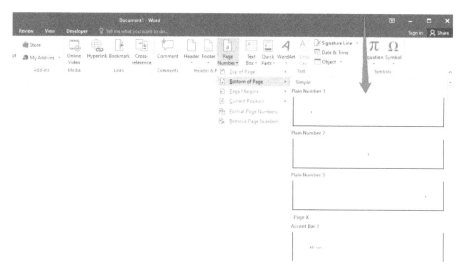

Changing page number formats

Change page number formats in the Page Number Format dialog box.

To show this dialog box, be certain you are in Print Layout view then double-click your header or footer and apply one of the following procedures to change page number formats.

> ➢ On the Header & Footer tab, click the Page Number button and select Format Page Numbers.

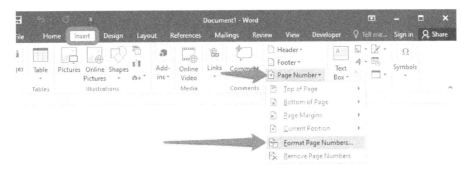

> ➢ On the insert tab, click the Page Number button and select Format Page Numbers.

In the Page Number Format dialog box, make your page numbers just so:

> ➢ **Selecting a different number format:** Unlock the Number Format drop-down menu and select a page-numbering format. You can use letters, roman numerals, or numbers.
> ➢ **Including chapter numbers in page numbers:** In case your document develops chapter numbers automatically from headings appointed in the same style, you can include the chapter number in the page number. Click the Include Chapter Number check box, select a style, and select a separator to move between the chapter number and page number.
> ➢ **Numbering each section separately:** Select the Start At option button to start counting pages afresh at each section in your document.
> ➢ **Start numbering pages at a number other than 1:** Select the Start At option button and input a number other than 1.

Placing Headers and Footers on Pages

A header is a little explanation that is displayed at the top of the page. Normally, headers comprise the page number and a title, and often the author's name is displayed in the header. A footer is similar to a header except that it displays beneath the page. These pages describe all you need to know about headers and footers. Meanwhile, here are the rules for operating them:

> ➢ **Changing to Print Layout view:** To input, read, edit, or delete headers and footers, you have to be in Print Layout view.
> ➢ **Showing the Header & Footer tab:** To show this tab after you have created a header or footer, change to Print Layout view and double-click outside the header or footer.
> ➢ **Closing the Header & Footer tab:** Click the Close Header and Footer button or double-click outside the header or footer.
> ➢ **Putting different headers and footers in the same document:** To modify headers or footers in the middle of a document, you need to create a new section.

Creating, editing, and removing headers and footers

Follow these steps to create, edit, and delete headers and footers:

- ➢ **Creating a header or footer:** On the Insert tab, select the Header or the Footer button, and pick a header or footer on the gallery. The gallery displays header or footers with preformatted page numbers, dates, and places to input a document title and author's name.
- ➢ **Selecting a different header or footer:** if you do not prefer the header or footer you select, double-click your header or footer to show it. Then click the Header or Footer button and select a new header or footer from the gallery.
- ➢ **Editing a header or footer:** Double-click the header or footer. The cursor transports into the header or footer so that you can input or format text. You can also click the Header or the Footer button and select Edit Header or Edit Footer on the drop-down menu.
- ➢ **Modifying the look of the header or footer:** Click a shape or text box in a header or footer and click a format tab to modify the shape or text box's size, color, and background.
- ➢ **Removing a header or footer:** On the Header & Footer tab, click the Header or Footer button and select Remove Header or Footer on the drop-down list.

Creating your header or footer for the gallery

When you click the Header or the Footer button on the Insert tab, a gallery displays with headers or footers. You can build or create your header or footer and position it on this gallery. For instance, build a header or footer with your business logo. After you design and build your header or footer, follow these steps to scrabble with it:

- ▪ **Placing a header or footer in the gallery:** Choose your header or footer by dragging across it or by clicking in the margin to its left. On the Header & Footer tab, pick the Quick Parts button and select Save Selection to Quick Part Gallery. Create New Building Block dialog box appears. Then enter a descriptive name for the header or footer, select Footers or Headers on the Gallery drop-down menu, and click OK.

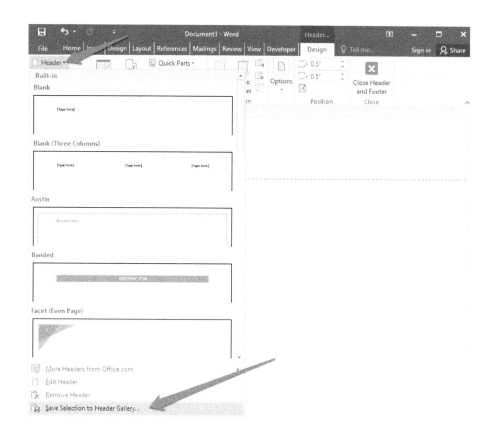

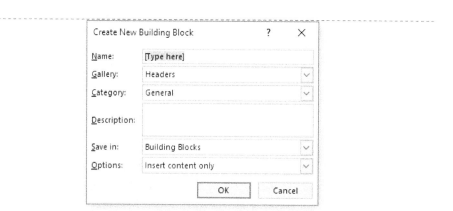

- **Inserting a header or footer you created:** On the Insert tab, click the Header or Footer button and select your header or footer in the gallery.
- **Removing and editing headers or footers:** Click the Insert tab, then click the Quick Parts button and select Building Blocks Organizer. The Building Blocks Organizer dialog box displays. Choose your header or footer and click the Delete button to extract it from the gallery or the Edit Properties button to modify its name, category assignment, or gallery assignment.

Modifying the Space Between Lines

To modify the spacing between lines, choose the lines whose spacing you want to modify, or place the cursor in a paragraph if you are modifying the line spacing throughout a paragraph. If you just want to start a document, you are set to move. On the home tab, click the Line and Paragraph Spacing button and select an option on the drop-down menu. To take the privilege of more line-spacing options, unlock the Paragraph dialog box, as displayed in the image below.

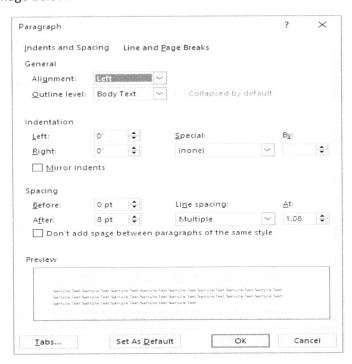

Apply either of these methods to unlock the Paragraph dialog box:

➤ Move to the Home tab and click the Paragraph group button

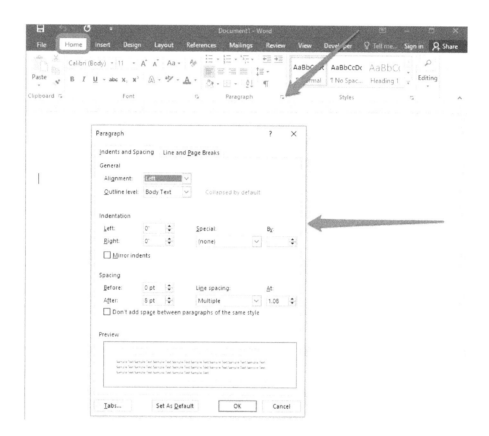

➤ On the Home tab, click the Line and Paragraph Spacing button and select Line Spacing Options on the drop-down menu.

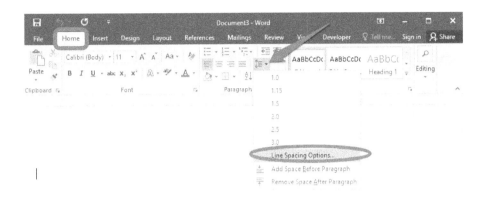

Other than single-, 1.5-, and double-spacing, the Paragraph dialog box provides these Line Spacing options:

> **Multiple:** Select this one and put a number in the At box to get triple-spaced, quintuple-, quadruple-, or any other number of spaced lines.
> **At Least:** Select this one if you want Word to modify for tall symbols or other unusual text. Word modify the lines but be certain there is, at minimum, the number of points you input in the At box between each line.
> **Exactly:** Select this one and input a number in the At box if you want a precise amount of space between lines.

Modifying the Space Between Paragraphs

Instead of pressing Enter to put a blank line between paragraphs, you can unlock the Paragraph dialog box and input a point-size measurement in the Before or After text box. The Before and After measurements place a precise amount of space before and after paragraphs.

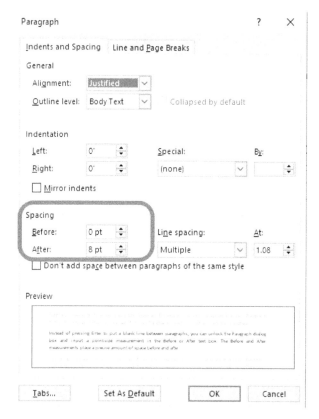

To tell the truth, the Before and After options are used with styles. But if you use the Before and After styles unsystematically, you may end up with large blank spaces between paragraphs.

Visit the Home tab and apply one of these methods to modify the amount of space between paragraphs:

➢ Click the Paragraph group button to unlock the Paragraph dialog box, then input point-size measurements in the Before and After boxes (or select Auto in these boxes to input one blank line between paragraphs in whatever your line-spacing preference is). The Don't Add Space Between Paragraphs of the Same Style check box informs Word to dismiss Before and After measurements if the previous or next paragraph is appointed the same style as the paragraph that the cursor is in.

➢ Click the Line and Paragraph Spacing button and select Add Space Before paragraph or Add Space after Paragraph on the drop-down menu. These commands position 10 points of blank space before or after the paragraph that the cursor is in.

Constructing Numbered and Bulleted Lists

Document is nothing without a list or two, Numbered lists are priceless in manuals and books. Apply bulleted lists when you are presenting alternatives to the reader. A bullet is a black, filled-in circle or other character. These pages describe numbered lists, bulleted lists, and multilevel lists.

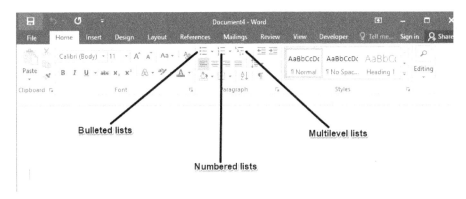

Simple numbered and bulleted lists

The fastest way to create a numbered or bulleted list is to click the Numbering or bullets button and begin to type the lists. Each time you press the Enter key, Word input the next number or another bullet.

Below are some tricks for dealing with lists:

> **Ending a list:** Press the Enter key twice after typing the final entry in the list.
> **Removing the numbers or bullets:** Choose the list and click the Numbering or Bullets button.
> **Modifying how far a list is indented:** Right-click anywhere in the list, select Adjust List Indents, and input a new measurement in the Text Indent box.

> **Starting a new list:** Presume that you want to begin a brand-new list immediately. Right-click the number Word entered and select Restart at 1 on the shortcut menu.

Creating lists of your own

To create a personal list, follow these steps for choosing unusual bullet characters and number formats:

❖ **Selecting a different numbering scheme:** On the Home tab, unlock the drop-down menu on the Numbering button and select a numbering scheme. You can also select the Define New Number Format dialog box. As displayed below, you notice where you can select number format, select a font for numbers, and bauble with number alignments.

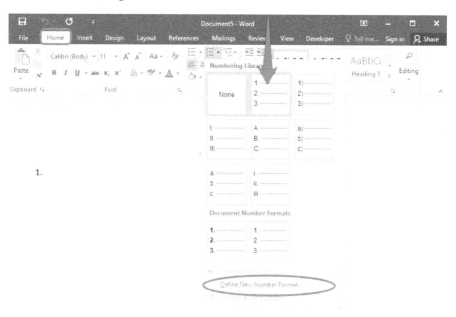

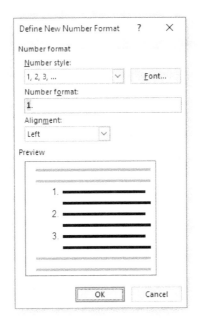

> **Selecting a different bullet character:** On the Home tab, unlock the drop-down menu on the Bullets button and select a different bullet character on the drop-down list. You can also select Define New Bullet to unlock the Define New Bullet dialog box, as displayed in the image below.

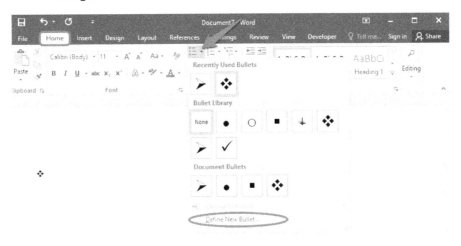

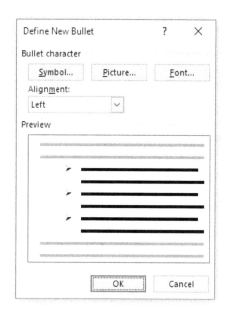

The dialog box also provides opportunities for indenting bullets and the text that follows them in unusual paths.

Operating a multilevel list

A multilevel list is a list with subordinate entries and is also known as a nested list. To create a multilevel list, follow these steps:

1. **On the Home tab, click the Multilevel list button and select what kind of list you need.**
   If you are not satisfied with any of the lists, you can select the Define New Multilevel list and create a fresh kind of list in the Define New Multilevel List dialog box.

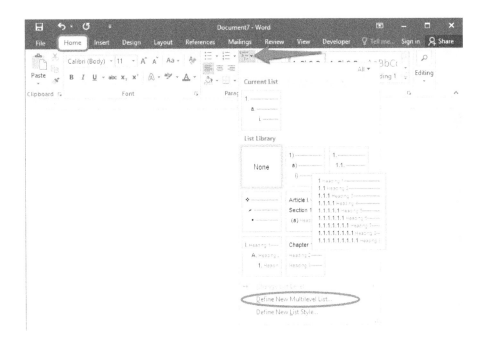

2. Input the items for the list, pressing Enter as you complete each one.

3. Choose a list item or items then click the Increase Indent button to make the items subordinate in the list; pick the Decrease Indent button to raise their rank in the list.

Chapter Three

Word Styles

Word style is the most important aspect of this book. A style is a collection of formatting commands gathered under one name. style saves time and makes documents look professional, you save yourself the stress of visiting many tabs and dialog boxes when you apply style. Headings appointed the same style- Heading1, for instance- all look alike.

Styles and templates

Every document comes with built-in styles that it acquires from the template with which it was created. You can create your style to complement styles from the template. A simple document constructed with the Blank Document template- a document that was constructed with a refined template comes with many styles.

Types of styles

In the Styles pane, the symbol close to each style name informs you what type of style you are bargaining with (click the Styles group button on the Home tab to unlock the Style pane). See the Styles pane as shown below.

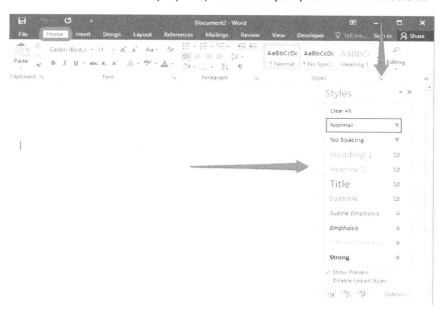

Word provides three style types:

- ➤ **Paragraph styles:** Specify the formatting of entire paragraphs. A paragraph style comprises these settings: tab, font, border, paragraph, language, bullets, text effects, and numbering. Paragraph styles are discernible by the paragraph symbol (¶).
- ➤ **Character styles:** Pertain to text, not to paragraphs. You choose text before you use a character style. Create a character style for foreign language text and text that is difficult to lay out. A character style comprises these settings: border, font, text effect, and language. Character styles are discernible by the letter α.
- ➤ **Linked (paragraph and character):** Use paragraph formats as well as text formats all over a paragraph. These styles are discernible by the paragraph symbol (¶) and also the letter α.

Using Styles to Text and Paragraphs

Word provides many ways to use a style, you will be asked to select the one that works best for you. These pages describe how to use a style and inform Word how to present style names in the numerous places where style names are presented for your desire and satisfaction.

Using a style

The first thing to do in using a style is to choose the part of your document that requires a style change, either text, a paragraph, or paragraphs, then apply or use the style with one of these methods:

- ➤ **Styles gallery:** On the Home tab, select a style in the Styles gallery. (you may need to click the Styles button first, depending on the size of your screen.) the image below displays where the Styles gallery is positioned.

> **Styles pane:** On the Home tab, click the Styles group button to unlock the Styles pane, and choose a style, as displayed in the image above select the show preview check box beneath the Styles pane to view formatted style names in the pane and obtain an idea of what the diverse styles are.

> **Apply Styles task pane:** Select a style on the Apply Styles task pane, see the Apply Style pane as displayed below.
> To show this task pane, move to the Home tab, and unlock the Styles gallery. Then select Apply Styles.

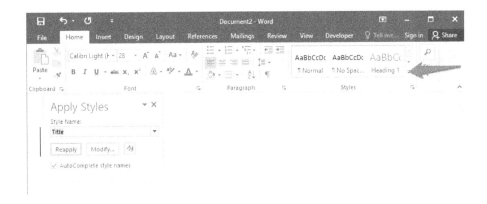

Testing with style sets

A style set is a slight variation of the styles in the template that you select when you construct your document. Style sets comprise Classic, Elegant, Fancy, and Modern. Selecting a style set provides a slightly different look on your document. To test with style sets, move to the Design tab and select an option in the Style Set gallery. To return to the original styles in a template, unlock the Style Set gallery and select Reset to the Default Style Set.

Selecting which style names display on the Style menus

One of the problems with using styles is looking for the right style to use in the Styles gallery, Styles pane, or Apply Styles task pane. All these can become congested with style names. To make finding and selecting style names comfortable, you can decide for yourself which names are displayed on the three style menus.

Styles pane and Apply Styles task pane

To choose for yourself which style names display in the Styles pane and Apply Styles task pane, click the Styles group button on the Home tab, then click the Options button in the Styles pane (located near the bottom of the pane). You notice the Style Pane Options dialog box, displayed below. Then select options to tell Word which style names display in the Styles pane and Styles task pane:

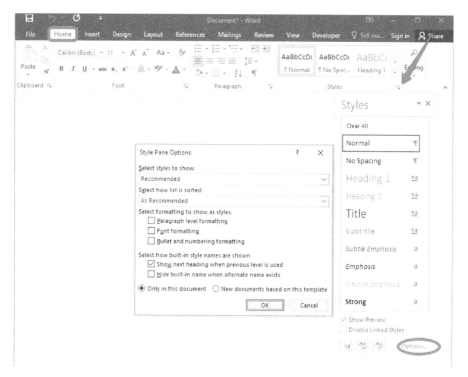

➢ **Select Styles to Show:** Select All Styles to display all style names. The other options position a subset of names in the window and task pane. Recommended style names are those that Microsoft believes you need most frequently.

➢ **Select How List Is Sorted:** Select an option to describe how to list styles Except for Based On, these options include, I think, self-explanatory. The Based On option lists styles in alphabetical order conceding to which style each style is founded on.

➢ **Select Formatting to Show As Styles:** Select options to tell which style to list- those that concern paragraph-level formatting, fonts, and bulleted and numbered lists.

➢ **Select How Built-In Style Names Are Shown:** Select options to declare how to deal with built-in styles, the uncertain styles that Word applies on its own when you construct tables of contents, and other self-generating lists.

> ➢ **Apply to this document or the template as well:** Click the Only In This Document option button to use your choices only to the document you are working on; select the New Documents Based on This Template option button to apply your selections to your document and to all future documents that you construct with the template you are using.

Creating a New Style

You can construct a new style by creating it from a paragraph or building it from the ground up. To do a detailed task, build it from the ground up because styles you create this way can be made aspect of the template you are presently working in and can be copied to other templates.

Creating a style from a paragraph

Follow these instructions to create a new style from a paragraph:

> ➢ **Click on a paragraph whose formatting you want to turn into a style.**
> ➢ **On the Home tab, unlock the Styles gallery and select Create a Style.**
> The Create New Style from Formatting dialog box appears.
> ➢ **Enter a name for your new style.**
> ➢ **Click OK.**

Creating a style from the ground up

To make a style functional in documents you will create in the future, make it an aspect of a template and build it from the ground up. In the Styles pane, click the New Style button (it is located beneath the pane). The Create New Style from Formatting dialog box appears, see it below.

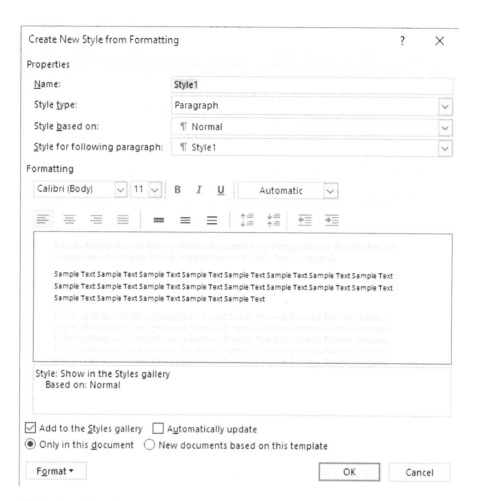

Fill in the dialog box and click OK.

Modifying a Style

Follow these instructions to modify a style that is not updated spontaneously:

1. Click in any table, list, or paragraph to which you are allocated the style; in case you want to modify a character style, choose the characters to which you have allocated the style.
2. In the Apply Style task pane, be certain that the name of the style that you want to modify is selected.

In case the right name is not chosen, choose it now in the Apply Styles task pane or the Styles pane.

3. **In the Styles pane, unlock the style's drop-down menu, right-click on any of the menus, and select Modify, as displayed below; then click the Modify button.**

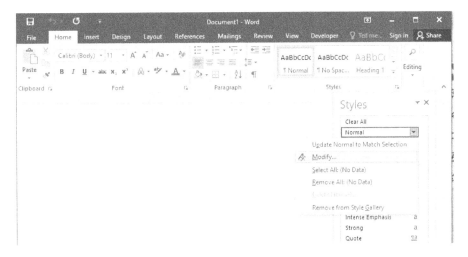

The Modify Style dialog box appears.

4. **Change the settings in the Modify Styles dialog box and click OK.**

Building and Managing Templates

One way to build a personal template is to begin by opening a document with numerous or all the styles you know and adore. When you save this document as a template, you pass along the styles in the document to the template, and you deliver yourself from the trouble of building styles for the template after you build it.

Follow these instructions to build a template on your own:

1. **Create a new document or unlock a document with styles that you can recycle.**
2. **On the File tab, select Save AS.**
   The Save As window unlocks.
3. **Click This PC.**
4. **Select the Browse button.**

The Save AS dialog box displays.

5. **Unlock the Save As Type menu and select Word Template.**
   The Save AS dialog box unlocks the folder where templates are kept on your computer.
6. **Impute a name for your template.**
7. **Click the Save button.**

Copying a style from one document to another

Copy a style from one document to another when you want the style on a one-time basis. Follow these instructions:

> **Choose a paragraph that was assigned the style you want to copy.**
> Be certain to choose the entire paragraph. If you want to copy a character style. Choose the text to which you have allotted the character style.

> **Press Ctrl+C or right-click and select Copy to copy the paragraph to the Clipboard.**

> **Change to the document you want to copy the style to and press Ctrl+V or click the Paste button on the Home tab**

> **Delete the text that you just copied to your document.**
> The style stays in the Styles pane and Styles gallery even if the text is deleted. You can ask for the style whenever you want it.

Copying Styles To A Template

Apply the Organizer to copy styles from a document to a template or from one template to another. When you are done making a style a part of a template, you can request the style in other documents. You can ask for it in each document you create with the template. Follow these instructions to copy a style into a template:

1. **Unlock the document or template with the styles you want to copy.**
2. **Click the Manage Styles button in the Styles pane.**
   This button can be found beneath the window. The Manage Styles dialog box displays

3. **Click the Import/Export button.**
   The organizer dialog box appears.
4. **Click the Close File button on the right side of the dialog box.**
   The button modifies names and becomes the Open File button.
5. **Click the Open File button and, in the Open dialog box, find and choose the template to which you want to copy styles; then, click the Open button.**
6. **In the Organizer dialog box, Ctrl+click to choose the names of styles on the left side of the dialog box that you want to copy to the template itemized on the right side of the dialog box.**
7. **Click the Copy button.**
   The names of the styles that you copied are displayed on the right side of the Organizer dialog box.
8. **Click the Close button and click Save when Word requests whether you want to save the new styles in the template.**

Opening a template so that you can change it

Follow these instructions to open a template in Word and be able to modify it:

❖ **On the File tab, select Open.**

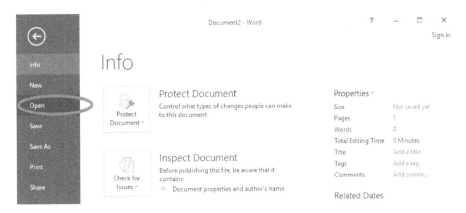

You notice the Open window.

❖ **Click This PC.**

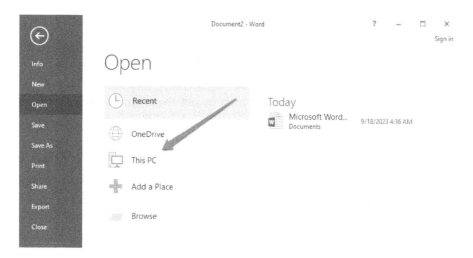

- ❖ **Click the Browse button.**
- ❖ **In the Open dialog box, move to the Templates folder where you store templates.**
- ❖ **Choose the template.**
- ❖ **Click the Open button.**

Modifying, deleting, and renaming styles in templates

Modify, delete, and rename styles in a template the same way you carry out those tasks to styles in a document (Modifying a Style has been explained earlier in this chapter). Nevertheless, in the Modify Style dialog box, choose the New Documents Based on This Template option button before clicking OK. Your style modification will apply to all documents you build in the future with your template. For the style modifications to take effect in documents you already created with your template, inform Word to spontaneously or automatically update document styles in those documents. Follow these instructions:

- ❖ **Save and close your template in case it is still open.**
- ❖ **Unlock a document that you want to update with the style modifications you made to the template.**
- ❖ **Move to the Developer tab.**
- ❖ **Click the Document Template button.**

The Templates and Add-ins dialog box opens.

❖ **Then choose the Automatically Update Document Styles check box.**

❖ **Click OK.**

Chapter four

Creating the Excellent Table

The best manner to present plenty of data at a time in Word is to do it in a table. Spectators can contrast and compare the data. As far as tables are concerned they have their terminology, the image below explains this terminology.

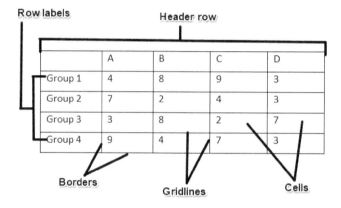

- ➤ **Row labels:** The labels in the first column that explain what is in the columns above.
- ➤ **Header row:** The name of the labels across the top row that describe what is in the columns above.
- ➤ **Borders:** The lines in the table that describe where the rows and columns are.
- ➤ **Gridlines:** The gray lines that display where the columns and rows are.
- ➤ **Cell:** The box that is formed where a row and column transect. Each cell holds one data item.

Creating a table

Beginning on the Insert tab, Word provides many ways to create a table:

- ➤ **Drag on the Table menu:** On the Insert tab, click the Table button, point in the drop-down list to the number of rows and columns you need, click, and release the mouse button, as displayed in the image below.

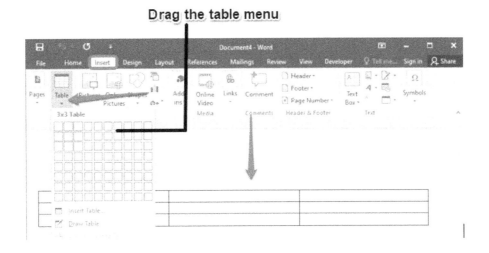

Drag the table menu

➢ **Use the Insert Table dialog box:** On the Insert tab, click the Table button and select Insert Table on the drop-down menu. The Insert Table dialog box comes into sight.

Use the Insert Table dialog box

Enter the number of columns and rows you want and click OK.

> **Draw a table:** On the Insert tab, click the Table button and select Draw Table on the drop-down menu. The pointer turns to a pencil and then uses the pencil to draw table borders, columns, and rows.

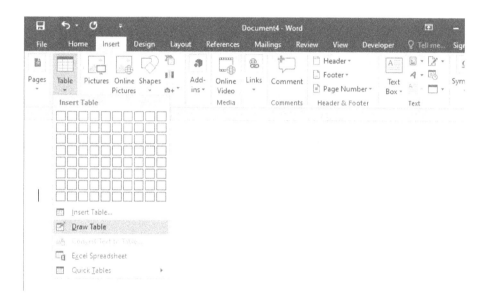

If you make an error while drawing the table, click the eraser button on the (Table) Layout tab and drag it across the aspects of the table the error is.

> **Create a quick table:** On the Insert tab, click the Table button and select Quick Tables on the drop-down menu. Then choose a ready-made table on the submenu. You must replace the sample data in the quick table with your data.

> ➢ **Construct a table from an Excel worksheet:** On the Insert tab, click the Table button, and select Excel Spreadsheet. An Excel worksheet displays, and you will notice Excel tabs and commands where Word tabs and commands used to be.

To delete a table, move to the (Table) Layout tab, click the Delete button, and select Delete Table on the drop-down menu.

Entering the Text and Numbers

You can start entering text and numbers after you have created the table. All you need to do is click in the cell and begin to type. Choose your table and apply these methods to make the burdensome task of entering table data a little stress-free:

➢ **Quickly changing a table's size:** Drag the size or bottom of a table to change its overall size. To make the table stretch from page margin to page margin, move to the (Table) Layout tab, click the AutoFit button, and select AutoFit Window.

➢ **Quickly Inserting a new row:** Click in the last column of the last row in your table and press the Tab key to quickly insert a new row beneath the table.

➢ **Selecting your preferred font and font size:** Entering table data is stress-free when you are working in a font and font size you like. Choose the table, visit the Home tab, and select a font and font size there. To choose a table move to the (Table Tools) Layout tab, click the Select button, and pick Select Table on the drop-down.

➢ **Moving a table:** Change to Print Layout view and drag the table selector (the square in the upper-left corner of the table).

Choosing Different Parts of a Table

Before you can alter, diddle, or reformat with table cells, columns, or rows, you need to choose them:

➢ **Choosing cells:** To choose a cell, click on it. You can choose numerous adjacent cells by dragging the pointer over them.

➢ **Choosing rows:** Shift the pointer to the left of the row and click when you notice the right-pointer arrow; click and drag to choose numerous rows.

➢ **Choosing columns:** Shift the pointer above the column and click when you notice the down-pointer arrow; click and drag to choose numerous columns.

➢ **Choosing a table:** Om the (Table) Layout tab, click the Select button, and pick Select Table on the drop-down list (or press Alt+5 on the numeric keypad).

Laying Out Your Table

In case you created numerous columns or rows for your table. Some columns may be too wide and others too narrow. In this situation, you need to change the table layout by deleting, inserting, and changing the size of rows and columns.

Changing the size of a table, columns, and rows

The quickest way to change the width of columns, the height of rows, and the size of a table itself is to stare at it and drag the mouse:

➤ **Column or row:** Shift the pointer onto a gridline or border, immediately the pointer changes into a double-headed arrow, and starts dragging. Tug and pull till the row or column is the right size.

➤ **A table:** Choose your table and apply one of these methods to change its size:

- **Table Properties dialog box:** On the (Table) Layout tab, click the Cell Size group button, and on the Table tab of the Table Properties dialog box, input a measurement in the Preferred Width text box.

- **Height and Width text boxes:** On the (Table) Layout tab, input measurements in the Height and Width text boxes.

- **Dragging:** Drag the top, side, or bottom of the table.

Amending column and row size

Adjusting columns and rows can be difficult in Word. Due to this reason, Word provides special commands on the (Table) Layout tab for resizing the width and height of columns and rows:

➤ **Making all columns the same width:** Click the Distribute Columns button to make all columns the same height. Choose rows before giving this command to make only the columns you choose the same width.

➤ **Making all rows the same height:** Click the Distribute Rows button to make all rows in the table the same height. Choose rows before clicking the button to make only the rows you choose the same height.

You can as well click the AutoFit button on the (Table) Layout tab, and take benefit of these commands on the drop-down list for dealing with rows and columns:

> **AutoFit Contents:** Make each column wide enough to house its widest entry.
> **AutoFit Window:** Extend the table so that it fits across the page between the right and left margins.
> **Fixed Column Width:** Fix the column widths at their present settings.

Inserting columns and rows

Word provides numerous ways to insert columns and rows. Some of the ways are:

On the (Table) Layout tab

Move to the (Table) Layout tab and follow these steps to insert and delete columns and rows:

> **Inserting columns:** Choose a column or columns and click the Insert Right or Insert Left button.
> **Inserting rows:** Choose a row or rows and click the Insert Above or Insert Below button.

To insert a row at the end of the table, shift the pointer into the last cell in the last row and press the Tab key.

Right-clicking

Follow these instructions to insert columns or rows by right-clicking:

- **Choose columns or rows.**
- **Right-click to show the mini-toolbar.**
  The image below shows the mini-toolbar you see immediately after you right-click a table.

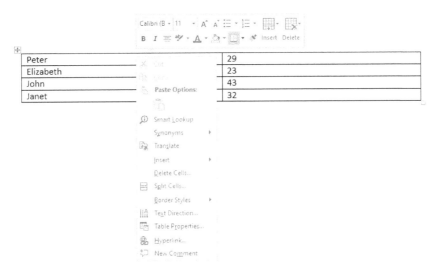

- **Click insert on the mini-toolbar.**
- **Select an Insert command (Right, Left, Above, or Below).**

One-Click Row and One-Click Column buttons

To insert one row or one column, click a One-Click button. The One-Click Column button displays when you shift the pointer between columns at the top of the table; the One-Click Row button displays when you shift the pointer between rows on the left side of the table. Click a One-Click button to insert one column or one row.

Deleting columns and rows

Move to the (Table) Layout tab and apply these methods to delete columns and rows:

- ➢ **Deleting columns:** Click on the column you want to delete, click the Delete button, and pick Delete Columns on the drop-down menu. Pick more than one column to delete more than one. (you can also right-click and select Delete Columns).

➢ **Deleting rows:** Click on the row you want to delete, click the Delete button, and select Delete Rows. Pick more than one row to delete more than one. (you can also right-click and select Delete Rows).

Pressing the Delete key after you choose a column or row deletes the data in the column or row, and not the column or row itself.

Moving columns and rows

To move a column or row, follow the steps below:

➢ **Choose the column or row you want to move.**
➢ **Right-click in the selection and select Cut on the shortcut menu.** The column or row is moved to the Clipboard.
➢ **Insert a new column or row where you want the column or row to be.**
➢ **Move the column or row:**

  ▪ **Column:** Click in the topmost cell in your new column and then click the Paste button (on the Home tab) or press Ctrl+V.
  ▪ **Row:** Click in the first column of the row you imputed and then click the Paste button (on the Home tab).

Aligning Text in Columns and Rows

Aligning text in columns and rows as to do with the positioning of text, in case you want the text to line up vertically and horizontally. Follow these instructions to align text in a table:

➢ **Choose the cell, rows, or columns, with text that you want to align (or choose your entire table).**
➢ **Move to the (Table) Layout tab.**
➢ **Click an Align button. (You may need to click the Alignment button first, depending on the size of your screen.)**

The image below displays where the Align buttons are on the (Table) Layout tab and how these options align text in a table.

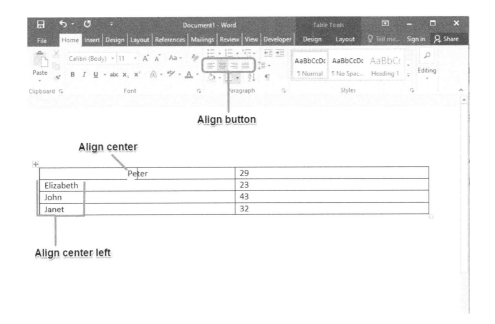

Merging and Splitting Cells

Choose the cells you want to merge or split, move to the (Table) Layout tab, and follow these steps to merge or split cells:

> **Merging cells:** Click the Merge Cells button. (You can also right-click and select Merge cells.)

> **Splitting cells:** Click the Split Cells button. (You can also right-click and select Split Cells.) in the Split Cells dialog box, state how many columns and rows you want to split the cell into, and then click OK.

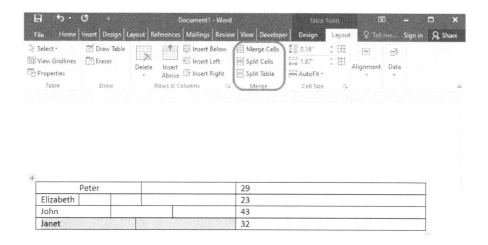

Peter			29
Elizabeth			23
John			43
Janet			32

Formatting Your Table

The quickest way to get a good-looking table is to select a table style in the Table Styles gallery, as displayed in the image below.

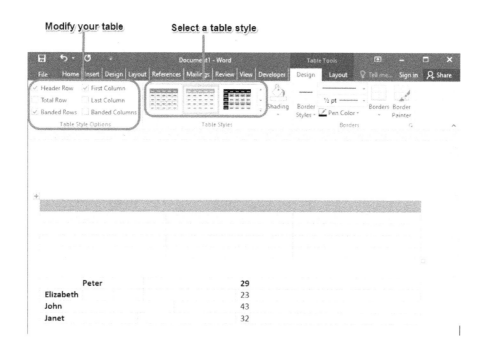

Peter	**29**
Elizabeth	23
John	43
Janet	32

A table style is a ready-made assortment of colors and border choices. You can deliver yourself from a lot of formatting stress by choosing a table style. After you choose a table style, you can modify it by selecting or deselecting check boxes in the Table Style Options group on the Table Design tab.

Click anywhere in your table and follow these instructions to select a table style:

> **Move to the Table Design tab.**
> **Unlock the Table Styles gallery and shift the pointer over table style choices to live-preview the table.**
> **Choose a table style.**

To remove a table style, unlock the Table Styles gallery and select Clear.

Decorating your table with borders and colors

Besides depending on a table style, you can assign an interior decorator on your own. The Table Design tab provides numerous commands that relate to table decoration. Apply these commands to shade table columns and rows and draw table borders.

Designing borders for your table

Follow these instructions to design a border for your table or aspect of your table:

> **Move to the Table Design tab.**
> **Select an aspect of your table that requires a new border.**
> To select the entire table, move to the (Table) Layout tab, click the Select button, and pick Select Table.
> **Create a look for the table borders you will draw or use.**
> Apply all or some of these methods to devise a border:
> - **Border style:** Unlock the drop-down list on the Border Styles button and select the border style that most resembles the one you want.
> - **Line style:** Unlock the Line Style drop-down menu and select style.
> - **Line weight:** Unlock the Line Weight drop-down menu and select a line thickness.

➢ **Unlock the drop-down list on the Borders button and select where to position borders on the part of the table you chose in step 2 above.**

You can also modify borders by clicking the Borders group button and making selections in the Borders and Shading dialog box, as displayed below.

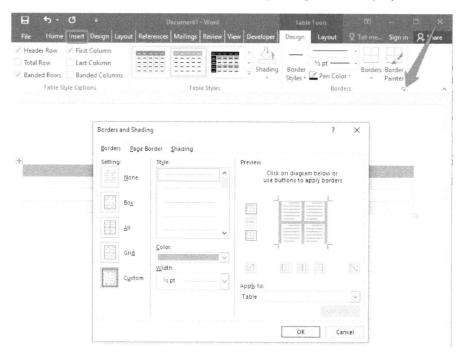

Choosing colors for columns, rows, or your table

Follow these instructions to decorate columns, rows, or your table a new color:

1. Choose the part of the table that requires a paint task.
2. In the Table Design tab, unlock the drop-down list on the Shading button and select a color.

Changing the direction of header row text

You can change the direction of the header row in a table in which the cell in the first row contains text and the cells beneath contain numbers, it will make it easier to read.

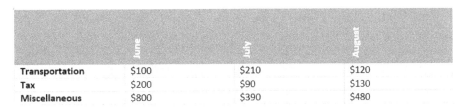

	June	July	August
Transportation	$100	$210	$120
Tax	$200	$90	$130
Miscellaneous	$800	$390	$480

Follow these instructions to change the direction of text on a table:

➢ **Choose the row that requires a change of text direction.**
➢ **Move to the (Table) Layout tab.**

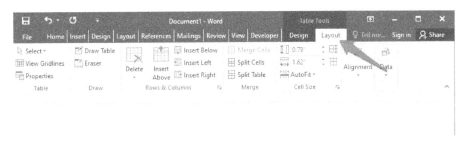

➢ **Click the Alignment button, then from the drop-down list keep clicking the Text Direction button until the text is in the position you want.**

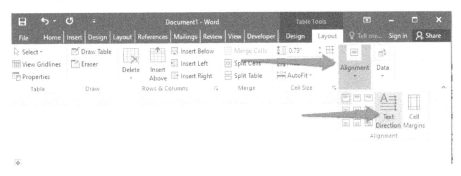

➢ **Modify the height of the row to make the vertical text fit.**
You can change or modify the height of a row by going to the (Table) Layout tab and putting a measurement in the Height box.

Wrapping text around a table

Follow these steps to wrap your table with text:

➢ On the (Table) Layout tab, click the Cell Size group button.

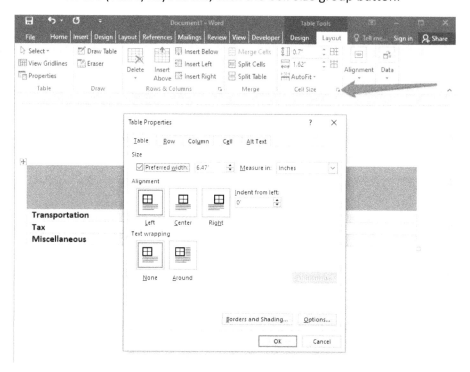

➢ On the table tab, beneath Text Wrapping, choose the Around option.

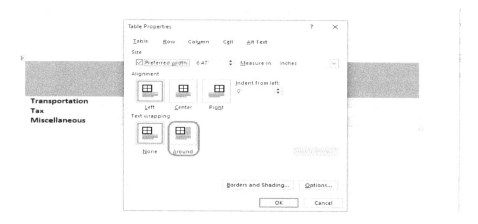

- ➢ **Click the Positioning button.** The Table Positioning dialog box displays.
- ➢ **Choose the Move with Text check box and click OK.** By choosing Move with Text, you make sure that the table remains with the surrounding text when you insert or delete text.
- ➢ **Click OK in the Table Properties dialog box.**

Making use of a picture as the table background

Positioning a graphic behind a table needs a fair bit of work, but the outcomes are well worth the effort. First, you insert the graphic and peradventure recolor it. Then you create the table. Finally, you make the table fit squarely on top of the graphic and peradventure group the objects together.

Follow the steps below to position a graphic behind a table:

1. **Insert the graphic, resize it, and format the graphic.** To insert a graphic, visit the Insert tab, click the pictures button, and select an option on the drop-down menu. To resize your picture, drag a selection handle; make the graphic as large as you want your table to be. To recolor a graphic, choose the picture format tab, click the Color button, and select an option.
2. **Click the Layout Options button and select Behind Text on the drop-down menu.** Selecting Behind Text informs Word to place the graphic behind the text. You can also move to the Picture Format tab, click the Wrap Text button, and select Behind Text.
3. **Insert the table and make it the same size as the graphic.** To modify the size of the table, drag a selection handle on its corner or side. Position the table adjacent to the graphic, but not right above it.
4. **On the Table Design tab, unlock the Table Styles gallery and select Clear.** With the table style out of the way, you can view the graphic clearly through your table.
5. **Input the data in the table, choose a font and font color, choose a border and border color, and align the text.**
6. **Shift the table directly on top of the graphic and then make the table and graphic the same size.**

Chapter Five

Taking Benefit of the Proofing Tools and Indexing a Document

This chapter explains how to proofread your work for misspellings, grammatical errors, and difficult writing it also explains how to index a document. It displays how to translate text and proof foreign language text. The F7 key is the key to the empire when it comes to proofing Word documents.

Here is the magic of pressing F7 and numerous key combinations:

> **F7:** Unlock the Editor to search for misspellings and grammatical errors.
> **Alt+F7:** Scroll to the next misspelling.
> **Shift+F7:** Unlock the Thesaurus.

Correcting Your Spelling Errors

Word accesses its dictionary when you input text in a document. To correct misspellings, you can either address them one at a time or start the spell checker and proof many pages at the same time.

Correcting misspellings one at a time

Using the one-at-a-time method of spell checker is one way of dealing with misspelled words. You can click or right-click each word that is underlined in red and select the correct spelling from the Spelling shortcut menu. Immediately after you select a word from the shortcut menu, it replaces the misspelling that you clicked.

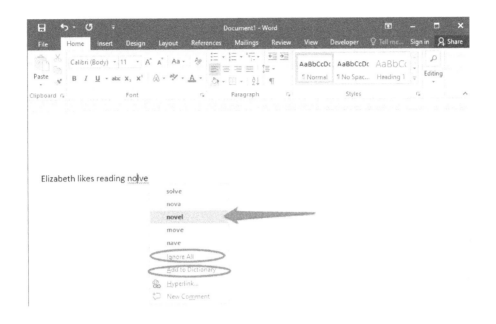

You can also click Ignore All on the Spelling shortcut menu to inform Word when a word is correctly spelled and should not be dried up. Or click Add to Dictionary, which adds the word to the Office spelling dictionary and states it is a correctly spelled word. Words imputed twice are also underlined in red, the Spelling shortcut menu provides the Delete Repeated Word option so that you can delete the second word.

Running a spell check

You can run a spell check on your work If you don't want to correct misspellings one at a time. Start your spell check with one of these techniques:

➤ Move to the Review tab and click the Editor button.
➤ On the status bar, click the Proofing Errors button. (Move the pointer over this button to see a pop-up message that informs you whether Word has located proofing errors in your document).
➤ Press F7.

The Editor task pane comes into sight. Beneath Corrections, it states how many spelling errors are in your document. Choose Spelling in the task pane to view suggestions for correcting a misspelling, the image below shows the Editor task pane.

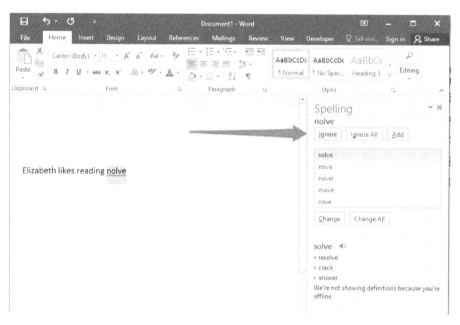

Here are options for correcting known misspellings in the Editor task pane:

> Choose the correct spelling.
> Click on the page you are working on and correct the misspelling; then click the Resume button in the Editor task Pane.

In case the word in question is not a misspelling, inform Word how to deal with the word by selecting one of these options:

> **Ignore All:** Ignores the misspelling all over the document you are working on and in all other open documents too.
> **Ignore Once:** Ignores this instance of the misspelling but stops on it again if the same misspelling displays later.
> **Add to Dictionary:** Add the misspelling to the Office spelling dictionary. By selecting this option, you inform Word that the misspelling is a genuine word or name.

> **Delete Repeated Word:** Deletes the second word in a couple of repeating words.

Preventing text from being spell-checked

Microsoft doesn't provide foreign language dictionaries is full waste of time. Follow these instructions to inform the spell checker to ignore text:

1. Choose the text.
2. In the Review tab, click the language button and select Set Proofing Language on the drop-down list.
3. Choose the Do Not check Spelling or Grammar check box.
4. Click OK.

Correcting Grammatical Errors

Word recognizes grammatical errors by double-underlining them in blue. Here are methods to correct grammatical errors:

> **Correct errors throughout a document:** Press F7 or click the Editor button on the Home tab. The Editor task pane unlocks. Beneath corrections, it accounts for how many grammatical errors are in your document. Choose Grammar in the task pane to visit a grammatical error in your document and, in case you want to, repair it by choosing an option beneath Suggestions.

> **Correct errors one at a time:** Click or right-click and select an option on the Grammar menu.

Finding and Replacing Text

Apply the Find command to locate a name or text passage. Apply it, twin, the influential Replace command, to find and replace a name or text passage all over a document. To know how useful, the Replace command is, assume that the organization you work for just changed its name and the old organization name is in many diverse places. By applying the Replace command, you can replace the old name with the new name all over a long document in a matter of seconds.

The fundamentals: Finding stray words and phrases

To find stray words, names, text passages, and formats, follow these fundamental steps:

1. **Press Ctrl+F or move to the Home tab and click the Find button.** You may have to click the Editing button before you can locate the Find button.

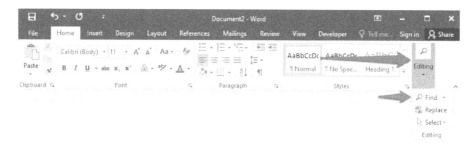

The Navigation pane displays so that you can enter search criteria in the Results tab.

2. **Enter the word or phrase in the search text box.**

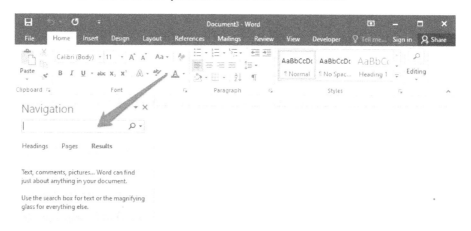

3. **If you want to conduct a narrow search, click the Search for More Things button- positioned at the right of the Search text box in the Navigation pane-and decide on the drop-down list.**

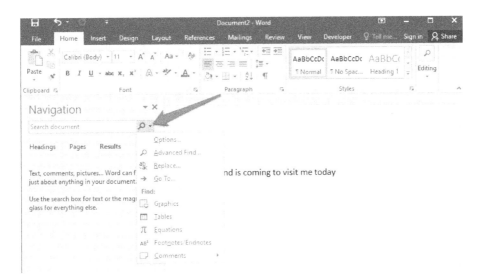

To narrow your search, click the Search for More Things button in the Navigation pane as displayed in the image above. Then select an option on the drop-down menu.

4. **Click an instance of the search term in the Navigation pane to scroll to a location in your document where the search term is positioned.**

Conducting a find-and-replace operation

Conducting a find-and-replace operation is the spitting image of conducting a Find operation. The image below displays the Replace dialog box, the place where you state what you want to find and what to replace it with.

To find and replace words, text passages, and names with the Find command, follow these instructions:

> **Move to the Home tab and click the Replace button or press Ctrl+H.**
> **Describe the text that requires replacing.**
> **Click the Find Next button.**
> **Enter the replacement text in the Replace With text box.**
> you can choose replacement text from the drop-down menu.
> **Either replace everything simultaneously or do it one at a time.**
> Select one of these button:
- Click Find Next and then either click Replace to make the replacement or Find Next to avoid it.
- Click Replace All to make all replacements immediately.

Finding the Right Word with the Thesaurus

You can make use of the Thesaurus to find synonyms for a word, begin by right-clicking the word and selecting Synonyms on the shortcut menu. To search for a good synonym, click the word in question and unlock the Thesaurus task pane with one of these methods:

> Press Shift+F7.

> Move to the Review tab and click the Thesaurus button.

> Right-click the word and select Synonyms-Thesaurus.

The Thesaurus task pane unlocks, as displayed in the image below. It provides a list of synonyms and sometimes comprises an antonym or two at the bottom.

My best friend is coming to vis

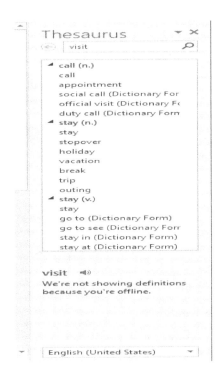

Proofing Text Written in a Foreign Language

Follow these instructions to tell Word that you will use a language or languages apart from English in your documents:

- ➢ **On the Review tab, click the Language button and select Language Preferences.**
- ➢ **Click the Add a Language button.**
- ➢ **Choose a language and click the Add button.**

   The name of the language you chose is displayed in the Word Options dialog box. If proofing tools are available for this language, the Proofing Available link displays next to the name of the language you chose.

- ➢ **Click the Proofing Available link.**

   Your browser unlocks a web page at Microsoft.com so that you can download the proofing tools.

- ➢ **Click the Download button and follow the instructions for downloading the language's proofing tools to your computer.**

Marking text as a foreign language text

The next thing is to inform the Office where in your document you are using a foreign language. After you mark the text as foreign language text, the Office can spell check it with the proper dictionaries.

Follow these instructions to mark text so that Office knows in which language it was written:

1. Choose the text that you wrote in a foreign language.
2. Visit the Review tab.
3. Click the Language button and select Set Proofing Language on the drop-down list.
4. Choose a language and click OK.

Translating Foreign Language Text

Follow these instructions to translate foreign language text:

1. **Choose the word or phrase that needs translation.**
2. **On the Review tab, click the Translate button and select a Translate option on the drop-down menu.**

The office provides these ways to translate words:

- **Translate Documents:** The Translator task pane unlocks, and if Word is able, the translation is made and entered into a new document. If Word can't discover the language that needs translating, unlock the From drop-down menu, select a language, and click the Translate button.
- **Translate Selection:** The Translator task panes unlocks. Click the insert button to replace the original text with the translated text. In case Word fails to discover the language that needs translating, unlock the From drop-down menu and select a different language.

Chapter Six

Desktop Publishing with Word

Sometimes years back Word processors were nothing more than overvalued typewriters. They were useful for typing and basic formatting, and not much else. But over the years, Microsoft Word has turned out to be a desktop-publishing program in its own right. This chapter describes some desktop-publishing features that can make your documents stand out in the crowd- columns, themes, text, boxes, watermarks, page borders, video, and drop caps.

Investigating with Themes

A theme is a ready-made, colorful design for headings and text. In case you want to investigate themes, theme colors, theme style sets, and theme fonts, more authority to you, but be prepared to click the Undo button and backtrack as you delve around for the right look for your document. On the Design tab, investigate themes, style sets, theme colors, and theme fonts.

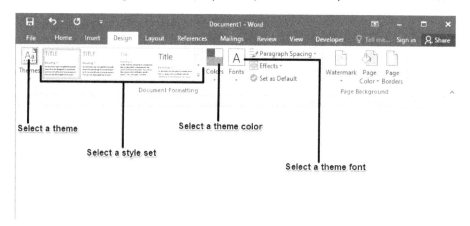

Commencing on the Design tab, follow these steps to investigate with themes:

> **Selecting a new theme:** Click the Themes button and select a theme on the drop-down list.
> **Selecting a new style set:** On the Themes Styles gallery, select a style set.

- ➢ **Selecting a new set of colors for your theme:** Click the Theme Colors button, slide the pointer across the diverse color sets on the drop-down list, and view what effect they have on your document.
- ➢ **Changing the fonts:** Click the Theme Fonts button and select a combination of fonts on the drop-down menu for the headings and text in your document.

Neatening Up Your Pages

You can play internal decoration with the pages of a document by placing a border around pages, wallowing color on pages, and taking advantage of the predesigned cover pages that Word offers for you. Continue reading if making the pages of your document a little lovelier interests you.

Decorating a page with a border

Word provides a means of decorating title pages, menus, certificates, and similar documents with a page border. Before you construct a border, position the cursor on the page where the border is to display. Position the cursor on the first page of a document if you want to place a border around only the first page. In case your document is separated into sections and you want to place borders around particular pages in a section, position the cursor in the section- either on the first page if you want the borders to go around it, or on the following page.

With the cursor in the right position, follow these instructions to decorate your page or pages with a border:

- ➢ **Visit the Design tab and click the Page Borders button.**
  You notice the Borders and Shading dialog box, as shown in the image below.

- ➢ **Beneath the Setting, select which kind of border you want.**
  Apply the None setting to remove borders.

> ➢ **On the Apply To drop-down list, inform Word which page in the document gets borders.**
> ➢ **Choose options to create the border you want and then click OK.**

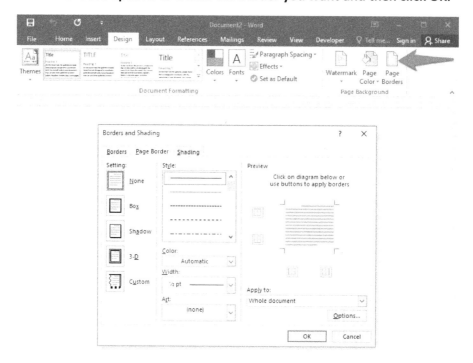

The Page Borders tab provides a bunch of tools for transforming a border:

> ➢ **Line for borders:** Beneath Style, scroll down the lists and select a line for the borders. You will discover interesting choices at the lowermost of the menu. Be sure to view the Preview window to see what your choice in this dialog box looks like.
> ➢ **Color for borders:** Unlock the Color drop-down menu and select a color for the border lines if you want a color border.
> ➢ **Width of borders:** Apply the Width drop-down menu to inform Word how wide the lines or artwork should be.
> ➢ **Borders on diverse sides of the page:** Use the four buttons in the Preview window to inform Word on which sides of the page to draw borders. Click these buttons to add or remove, as you desire.
> ➢ **Distance from edge of page:** Click the Options button and fill in the Border and Shading Options dialog box if you want to get precise

about how close the borders can come to the edge of the page or pages.

➢ **Artwork for borders:** Unlock the Art drop-down menu and select a symbol, illustration, or star. Or other artwork, if that is what you need for the borders. You will discover some ornate choices at the bottom of the long list.

Placing a background color on pages

To polish a page with a background color or gradient color mixture, visit the Design tab, click the Page Color button, and select a color on the drop-down menu. Select Fill Effects to unlock the Fill Effects dialog box and apply gradient color mixtures or patterns to the pages.

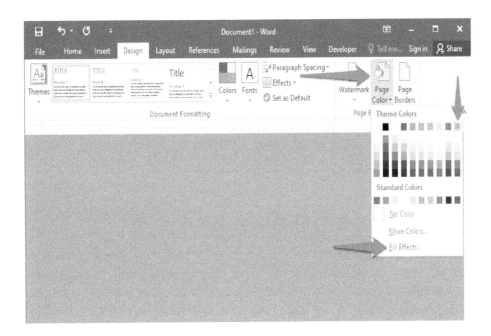

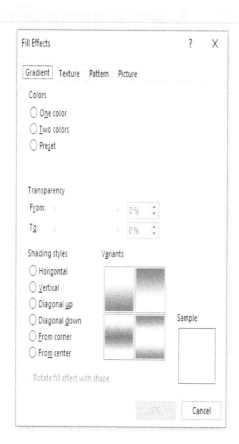

Obtaining Word's help with cover letters

Writing and designing a cover page for a letter, resume, or report is a task. Word can't decree a cover page for you, but it can offer a handsome preformatted cover page that looks good at the front of a report or article. To get ready-made cover pages visit the Insert tab, then click the Pages button. The image below shows examples of ready-made cover pages.

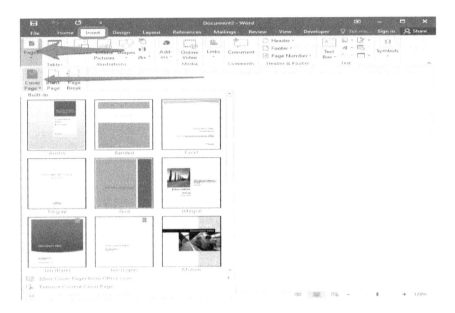

Making Use of Photos, Shapes, Diagrams, and Charts

> **Photos:** The photo makes a document energetic. They add a little color to documents.

> **Shapes and lines:** Shapes and lines can also demonstrate ideas and concepts. You can also apply them for decorating purposes in Word documents.

> **Diagrams:** A diagram permits readers to quickly grasp an idea, concept, or relationship. Instead of explaining non-concrete ideas. You can describe it in a diagram.

> **Charts:** A chart is an exceptional way to present data for contrast purposes.

Working with the Drawing Canvas

Drawing lines and shapes is difficult unless you draw them on the drawing canvas. The drawing canvas makes working with objects on a page, most especially shapes and lines, that much stress-free.

Follow these instructions to create a drawing canvas for holding lines and shapes:

85

1. **Position the cursor where you want the drawing canvas to be.**
2. **Click the Insert tab or the Draw tab.**
3. **Create the drawing canvas.**

How to create the drawing canvas depends on where you are:

➢ **Insert tab:** Click the Shapes button and select New Drawing Canvas (the lowermost option on the drop-down menu).

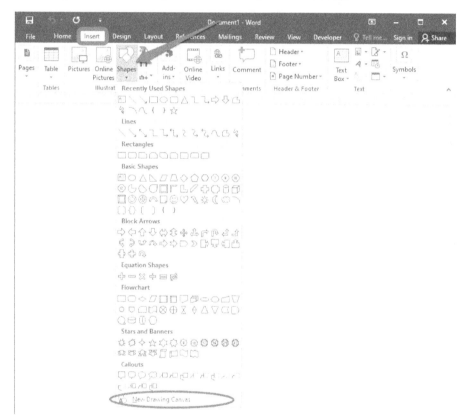

➢ **Draw tab:** Click the Drawing Canvas button.

The drawing canvas is an object in its own right. You can wrap text all over it, then give it an outline, and color fill. See the image displayed below.

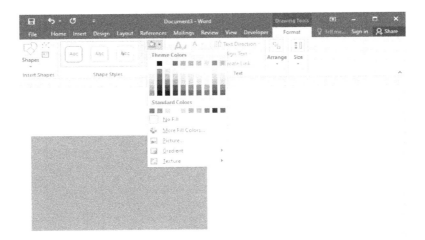

Wrapping text around an object

You can wrap text around an object in diverse ways. Select the object you want to wrap text around and use one of these methods to wrap text around the object:

- ➤ Click the Layout Options button and select an option on the drop-down menu.
- ➤ On the Format or Layout tab, click the Wrap Text button and select an option on the drop-down list. Depending on the size of your screen, you may have to click the Arrange button first.
- ➤ Unlock the Layout dialog box, move to the Text Wrapping tab, and select a wrapping style and side around which to wrap text. To unlock the Layout dialog box:
  - Click the Layout Options button (to the right of the object) and click the See More link on the drop-down menu.
  - Click the Wrap Text button and select More Layout Options on the drop-down menu.

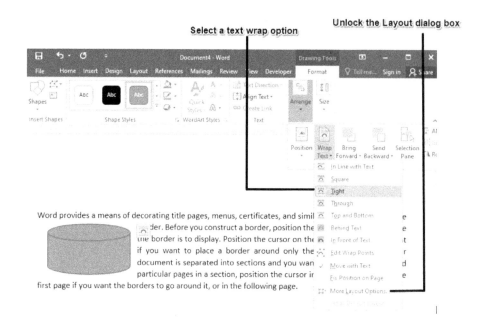

Word provides a means of decorating title pages, menus, certificates, and simil der. Before you construct a border, position the une border is to display. Position the cursor on the if you want to place a border around only the document is separated into sections and you wan particular pages in a section, position the cursor ir first page if you want the borders to go around it, or in the following page.

Placing an object on a page

To place an object in a Word page, you can drag it to a new position. Dragging means choosing the object, moving the pointer across its perimeter, clicking when you notice the four-headed arrow, and sliding the object to a new position. To make placing objects on a page comfortable, Word provides Position commands for moving objects to a particular place on the page. For instance, you can position an object directly in a corner or center of the page

Choose your object, move to the Layout or Format tab, and apply one of these methods to shift or move your object exactly into place:

➢ Click the Position button and select More Layout Options on the drop-down menu, or click the Size group button on the Format tab and select the Position tab in the Layout dialog box. Then select position options. Visit the Layout dialog box in case you want to position objects in the very same place on diverse pages.

➢ Click the Position button and select a With Text Wrapping option on the drop-down list, as displayed below. These options place an object exactly in a corner, a side, or the middle of the page.

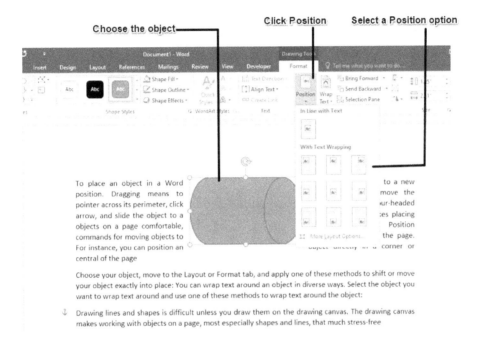

To place an object in a Word position. Dragging means to pointer across its perimeter, click arrow, and slide the object to a objects on a page comfortable, commands for moving objects to For instance, you can position an central of the page

to a new move the ur-headed es placing Position the page.

Choose your object, move to the Layout or Format tab, and apply one of these methods to shift or move your object exactly into place: You can wrap text around an object in diverse ways. Select the object you want to wrap text around and use one of these methods to wrap text around the object:

⬇ Drawing lines and shapes is difficult unless you draw them on the drawing canvas. The drawing canvas makes working with objects on a page, most especially shapes and lines, that much stress-free

Working with Text Boxes

Input text in a text box when you want a notice to stand out on the page. Like other objects, text boxes can be filled with color, shaded, and given borders, you can also lay them over graphics to make for exciting effects. To insert a text box, visit the Insert tab, click the Text Box button, and apply one of these methods:

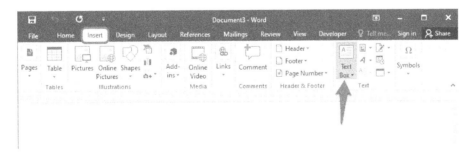

- ➢ **Select a ready-made text box:** Scroll in the drop-down list and select a preformatted text box.

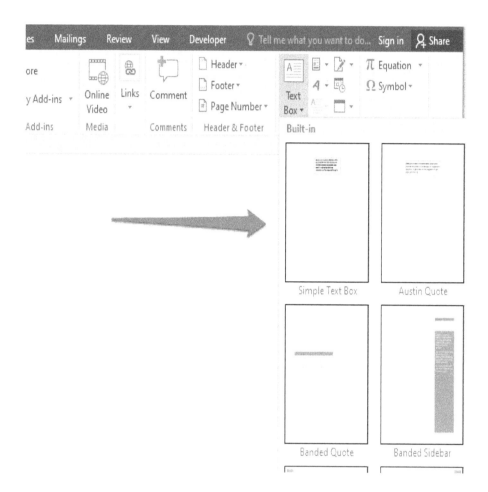

- ➢ **Draw a conventional text box:** Choose Draw Text Box on the drop-down menu, and then click and drag to draw the text box. Lines reveal to you how large it will be when you release the mouse button.

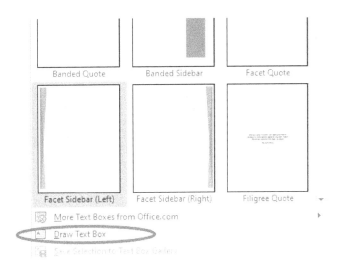

After you have inserted the text box, you can type text in it and call on all the formatting commands on the (Drawing) Format tab.

Dropping in a Drop Cap

A drop cap is a big capital letter that "drops" into the text. Drop caps are displayed at the beginning of chapters in many books. See the image below.

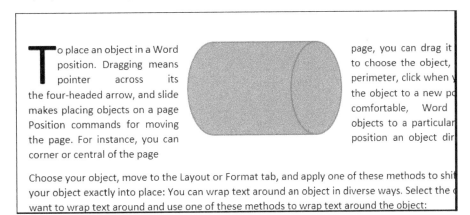

To construct a drop cap, begin by clicking anywhere in the paragraph whose first letter you want to drop. In case you want to drop many characters at the beginning of the paragraph, choose the characters. Then visit the Insert tab, click the Drop Cap button, and select Dropped or Drop Cap Options.

Selecting Drop Cap Options unlocks the Drop Cap dialog box. See the Drop Cap dialog box below.

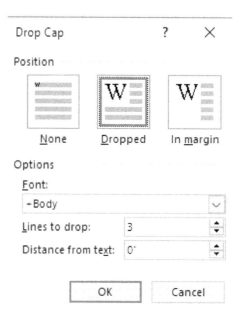

Then experiment with these options:

> ➢ **Position:** Select which kind of drop cap you want.
> ➢ **Font:** Select a font from the Font drop-down list. Pick a different font from the text in the paragraph.
> ➢ **Lines to Drop:** Input the number of text lines to drop the letter.
> ➢ **Distance from Text:** Keep the 0 settings unless you are dropping a *t*, 2, or other skinny or number.

Click the Drop Cap button and select None to remove a drop cap.

Watermarking for the Elegant Effect

A watermark is a pale image or set of words displayed behind text on each page of a document. Watermarks are one of the stress-free formatting tricks to achieve in Word.

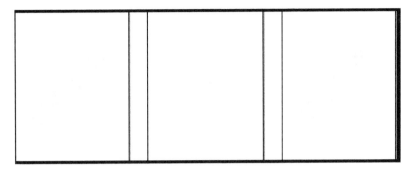

To generate watermarks for every page of a document, visit the Design tab and click the Watermark button. From the drop-down menu, generate your watermark:

> **Prefabricated text watermark:** Scroll down the list and select an option. You will discover trustworthy, urgent, and other text watermarks.

> **Picture watermark:** Select Custom Watermark, and in the Printed Watermark dialog box, click the Picture Watermark option button. Then pick the Select Picture button. In the Insert button, choose a graphics file to use for the watermark and click the Insert button. Return to the Printed Watermark dialog box, select or input size for the graphic on the Scale drop-down list. See the Printed Watermark dialog box below.

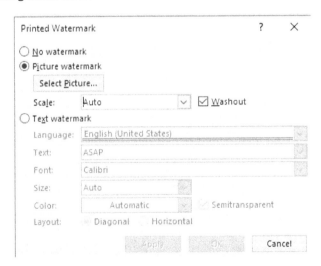

➢ **Text watermark:** Select Custom Watermark and, in the Printed Watermark dialog box, click the Text Watermark option button. Type a word or two in the Test box. Select a font, size, color, and layout for the words.

Landscape documents

A landscape document is one in which the page is broader than it is lengthy. Constructing a landscape document is sometimes a decent idea because a landscape document stands out from the usual crowd of portrait documents and sometimes printing in landscape mode is essential to fit text, graphics, and tables on a single page.

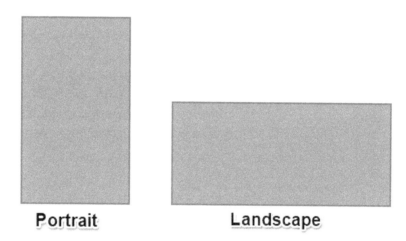

Portrait   **Landscape**

To turn some pages into landscape pages, construct a section for the pages that need to be in landscape mode and click on the section (Chapter 2 of this book describes the section). Beginning on the Layout tab, apply these methods to change the page orientation:

➢ **Portrait pages:** Click the Orientation button and select Portrait on the drop-down list.
➢ **Landscape pages:** Click the Orientation button and select Landscape on the drop-down list.

Printing on Different Size Paper

You don't need to print exclusively on standard 8.5 x 11 paper; you can print on legal-size paper, A4 paper, and other sizes of paper. Move to the Layout tab and apply one of these methods to modify the size of the paper on which you propose to print a document:

> Click the Size button and select More Paper Sizes. You notice the Paper tab in the Page Setup dialog box. Select a setting on the Paper size drop-down menu. If none of the settings satisfy you, input your settings in the Width and Height text boxes.
> Click the Size button and select an option on the drop-down list.

Displaying Online Video in a Document

When words and pictures cannot perform the task, you can make video a part of your document with the Online Video command. This command creates a link between your document and a video on the Internet. After you create the link, the first frame of the video is displayed in the Word document.

Before you input a video, visit online to the video you want to input and copy its URL (its address) to the Clipboard. Then follow these instructions to input the video in your document:

> **On the Insert tab, click the Online Video button.**

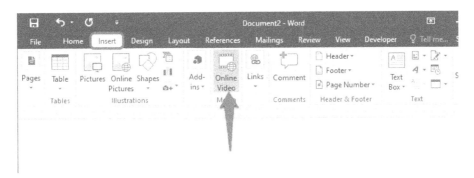

The insert a video dialog box comes into sight.

> **Paste the URL you copied into the textbox.**

The comfortable way to do that is to click in the textbox and press Ctrl+V.

➢ **Click the Insert button.**

The video lands in your Word document.

CONCLUSION

I am very sure you now have a full understanding of how to use Microsoft Word after going through every part of this book, I am sure you can now Start Word and navigate your way around the ribbon tab, and I also believe you now know some quick methods for using word, laying out text and pages, word style, taking advantage of the proofing tools and also how to create the perfect table, and so on.

INDEX

A

Aligning, 60
article, 82

B

bookmarks, 15
Borders, 52
Building Block, 29

C

canvas, 83
columns, 54
Computerized, 17

D

data, 52
Deleting rows, 60
desktop-publishing, 78
dialog, 25
documents, 6
Draft view, 10

E

eyeball, 23

F

Find command, 71
find-and-replace, 73
Footer tab, 29
foreign language, 76

G

gradient, 81

grammatical, 68
graphics, 21

H

headers, 19
height, 57

I

Indent, 23

M

Margin, 21
merge, 61
misspellings, 68
modify, 5

N

newspaper, 19
Numbering, 25
numerous, 47

P

Paragraph, 19
Paragraph Spacing button, 32
perimeter, 86
pointer, 59
preformatted, 82
Print Layout, 9
proofread, 9

R

replaces, 68
Review tab, 74
Ribbon, 6
Roman, 25

S

screen, 5
Section, 20
spell check, 69
Split Cells, 61
Style Set Gallery, 43
symbol, 41

T

Table, 53
task pane, 42
template, 8

text box, 87
Text Wrapping tab, 85
the Insert tab, 29
Theme Colors, 79
title pages, 79

W

watermark, 90
Width, 57
window, 9
Word style, 40
Wrapping text, 66

www.ingramcontent.com/pod-product-compliance
Lightning Source LLC
LaVergne TN
LVHW081801050326
832903LV00027B/2038